GOD TAKE THIS CUP FROM ME
But Not My Will

God Will Change Your Tragedy Into Purpose

PROPHETESS DO... MORRIS

God Take This Cup Away From Me

By Prophetess Dolly Morris

Cover Created & Designed by Dolly Morris

Logo Designs by Andre M. Saunders/Jess Zimmerman

Editor: Anelda L. Attaway

© 2020 Dolly Morris

ISBN 978-1-7357874-6-6

Library of Congress Control Number: 2020921259

All rights reserved. This book is protected by the copyright laws of the United States of America. This book may not be copied or reprinted for commercial gain or profit. The use of short quotations or occasional page copying for personal or group study is permitted and encouraged. Permission will be granted upon request. This book is for Worldwide Distribution and printed in the United States of America, published by Jazzy Kitty Publications utilizing Microsoft Publishing Software. Scriptures are from the Holy Bible, NIV or NKJV version. The "devil" is lowercased to honor God.

DEDICATIONS

This book is dedicated to the memory of my mother, Lula Green, and the victims that lost their lives to the coronavirus known as COVID-19.

ACKNOWLEDGMENTS

First and foremost, I want to thank my Lord and Savior, Jesus Christ. Thank God for the Holy Spirit's inspiration to let me know that this is the season to bring this book forth.

Thank God for my family, who always support every project that I put my hands to do.

A special thanks to my husband, Marvin Morris Jr., and my wonderful children Tasario, Chrystal, and Marvin 3rd, Shelita, and Marshona for all their support and assistance in this project.

Thank you, Lula Green, for allowing me the privilege of being your daughter. I would always say if God gave me a choice to pick my mother, I could not have picked anyone greater. You were amazing. Whatever I do now, it's with you in mind. I love you.

I want to thank my auntie Doretha Smith and cousin Ethel Ross for taking care of my mother during her time on earth.

Thanks to Monique Cornish and Sodonia Worthy for their support and always being available to share their wisdom and spiritual advice.

I want to thank my spiritual leaders and in-laws, Bishop Marvin Morris Sr., and First Lady Lorriane Morris, for all you have poured into my life.

Thank you, Booker St COG family, for your encouragement.

Thank you, Women Birthing A Nation Women, for pouring into my life when at times, I felt so empty. You were there holding my arms up when I had no strength to give.

Thank you, Chrystal and Marvin, for the photos.

Last but not least, thanks, Jazzy Kitty Publications, for the awesome opportunity for publishing my book. It has been an awesome experience.

There are no words that I could say to express how I truly feel deep within my heart. However, I must let you all know how grateful I am to have each of you as a part of my life. Please know that each of you listed in my acknowledgments holds a special place in my heart; now, forever, and always.

I love you all, and may God continue to bless each of you.

TABLE OF CONTENTS

INTRODUCTION i
CHAPTER 1 – Answering the Call 01
CHAPTER 2 – Have You Tried My Servant? 10
CHAPTER 3 – Know Who You Are in God 14
CHAPTER 4 – An Intimate Relationship with God 17
CHAPTER 5 – Will You Go 20
CHAPTER 6 – It Will Cost You Something 23
THE CONCLUSION 35
ABOUT THE AUTHOR 37

INTRODUCTION

Have you ever been in a place where the light seems to have been dimmed? Have you ever been in a place in life where you can't see the light of day? You felt like God has left you in a dark room and expect you to find a way to escape on your strength and wisdom. You're crying out to God, asking Him the question, "God! Where are you?" I want you to know that you are not alone. As Christians, whether we admit it or not, we have all been there.

In this Part 1 Series of God Take This Cup Away From Me, I will share my testimony of how God's grace and mercy allowed me to triumph over those things that the devil thought would kill me. My prayer is that you will realize that, like a good Father, God will not destroy you. However, He will allow things to take place in our lives to mold us into vessels of honor to be used for His glory. Therefore, you must trust the process, be patient, and allow the Holy Spirit to be the light to guide you into the perfect plan of God.

Psalm 119:105, Your word is a lamp for my feet, a light on my path.

When you have reached the point that you can't handle one more trial or failure, remember **1 Corinthians 10:13, No temptation has overtaken you except what is common to**

mankind. And God is faithful, He will not let you be tempted beyond what you can bear.

The Bible talks about the three Hebrew boys and how God allowed them to be put in the fiery furnace. Even though they were put in the furnace, God didn't allow them to be consumed. The fire will come into your life, and you will have to experience the heat. Just know that God will be in the fire with you. When you help a child learn to walk or ride a bike, you will hold them. There will come a time when you will let them go. They may fall until they catch on, but they will get up and try again. Often, this is how the lessons of life will be. We may fall, but God expects us to get back up and try again. There have been times in my life that I made decisions that caused me to not only fail God but fail people that believed and trusted in me. Praise God for His awesome mercy and grace that allows us new opportunities every day.

Follow me on my journey of going through the fire and coming out not smelling like smoke.

CHAPTER 1

Answering the Call

I remember telling myself there's got to be more to life than this. It's Wednesday night, and I just got off from a long day at the salon. I picked up the phone and called the crew, asking what time we are going to the club tonight. We set a time.

"Ok, Ladies I will meet you there," I said.

I thought to myself, *"It's gonna be on tonight."*

I'm in the mirror singing as I'm getting dressed. Singing something like, *"It's Ladies' Night and the feeling's right. Oh yes, it's Ladies' Night, Oh, what a night or I'm every woman."*

When I get to the club, the girls are there to greet me. We head to the bar to get our drink on. After about an hour of getting our drinks, it's time to hit the dance floor.

After an hour of burning the floor and the settling of alcoholic beverages, the stench of armpits and smell of cigarettes almost made me sick. This routine took place Wednesday through Sunday every week, like clockwork. We would have a ball. However, every night I found myself disappointed in the midst of the smoke-filled and musty smelling room. I would sit at the table in the corner, staring out at the crowd that seemed to be dancing in slow motion asking myself the question, *"What am I doing here?"* It didn't matter how good of a time we had; there was always a void at the end of the night. I remember getting the phone call from my best friend, Sodonia.

She said, "Girl, I got saved!"

"Saved from what?" I thought to myself.

"I gave my life to the Lord," Sodonia said.

"OMG! Girl, I'm happy for you," I said, but not understanding to the fullness what that meant.

After talking about her new redemption and how awesome she felt, the conversation ended, and I hung up the phone. I realized something was different about her voice. She sounds so alive and excited. Little did I know that my ride or die, my friend's life was headed in a different direction.

I continued the party life. I was looking for love in all the wrong places. I was looking for something or someone to feel this empty feeling that nothing was enough to erase. Regardless what I did the emptiness was still there. I began to drink more frequently. I was no longer just drinking on weekends; I was drinking every day of the week. My life seemed to be spiraling out of control. The club life began getting dangerous. Gangs started to pop up everywhere, and young boys wanted to claim their territory. They wanted to make that quick money selling drugs. Going out trying to have a good time at the club started becoming like a marathon, dashing to save your life. I remember one night at the club having to get under the table because of the sound of a gunshot inside a night club with one way out. I swore if I got out of there, I was done living that lifestyle. Of course, that thought shot passed by my head as quickly as that bullet did. Instead of changing my lifestyle, we just changed the location.

This behavior went on for a few more months. I was still trying to fill the void that I was feeling, and man, was I missing my girl Sodonia. So, I decided to give her a call.

I asked her, "Are you still saved?" She began to tell me how awesome it was being saved and how she wished she had done this a long time ago.

"Yeah, Yeah," I was thinking to myself.

This went on for probably six months. Each time I called Sadonia, I was hoping to hear her say, "Where are we going tonight?"

Instead, it was "Yeah, Girl; I love Jesus."

However, she never pressured or judged me. Whenever we talked, I witnessed the transformation and the love of God in her life.

After six months of waiting and hoping that she would change her mind to come back to the streets, the response was always the same. I was watching her and the transformation that had taken place. There was no wearing her down, LOL.

I said to myself, *"I'm gonna call one last time."*

I called her, and I asked, "You still saved?"

She said, "Yes."

Out of nowhere, I said, "Maybe, I'll go with you one day."

She said, "Yeah, you should."

Supposed Sodonia had changed her mind? Remember that someone is watching your life. Make sure you are portraying Christ. We had made arrangements to meet up so I could go to church with her. I'm not sure what happened. I guess that old devil didn't want that divine appointment to take place.

About a couple of weeks later, I was watching TBN. Don't ask me why, but this minister came on, and he was preaching up something fierce. I still remember the sermon today; he was ministering on Cain and Abel. I wasn't raised in the church, but it was something about the message that began to draw me in. I didn't understand what the preacher was saying, but it touched a part of me that had never been touched before. It was a feeling no person, no drug, nor alcohol beverage could ever make me feel. I began to cry like a baby.

The minister said at the end of the message, "If you want to give your life to Christ, you can do it right where you are."

I repeated the Sinner's Prayer and gave my life to Christ; I didn't know a lot about this journey. Though I had it set in my head, I had to be in church to be saved. There was no way it was that easy. I ran to my mom's church, went to the altar, and once again said the Sinner's Prayer. I wanted to make sure TD Jakes knew what he was saying when he said it was that easy, LOL. Jesus saved me that day. My friend was right; it is the best thing that I have ever done. The love I feel is awesome. The feeling of emptiness is sometimes there. However, unlike before, whenever I draw close to Him, He restores, refills, and reconciles me back to the Father. That's such a precious gift. If you find yourself in a place of emptiness, loneliness, despair, or hopelessness, Salvation is that easy. Repeat this prayer after me:

"Dear Heavenly Father,

Forgive me for my sins. I repent of them all. I accept You into my life today. I believe that Your Son died on the cross for me and resurrected on the third day to give me eternal life. I confess my faith in Him and accept Him as my personal Savior." You are now saved. You are a servant of the most High God. It is that easy.

I had been in a relationship for about two years with my now-husband. I remember when Marvin came in, and I said to him, "I got saved today." He looked at me as to say, yeah, right. I was so excited about my decision. I just wanted God to be pleased with me. By this time, Marvin and I were in somewhat of a committed relationship; we were living together, as some would say, playing house. He was not buying the cow but getting the milk for free. The old folks would say, living in sin. I knew if I were going to do the right thing, I would have to go home. I knew God was soon going to get tired of my excuses. I also knew Marvin was gonna get tired of them, too, because he wasn't saved. After all, I have been intimate with this man for two years. Now, I'm saying I'm saved and no fornicating. It wasn't like he didn't know we couldn't fornicate. He was a preacher's kid, a PK, so he knew.

He said, "God understands we've been in a relationship for two years. He doesn't expect you just to leave. It's not like we are not gonna get married someday."

The thought in the back of my mind was, *"If I leave, He will get someone else or at least be with someone else."*

So, I was persuaded one last time to indulge in sin. It was hard to persuade me too. I fought a good fight, LOL. Seriously though,

I was so convicted that I told him I was leaving; I'm going home. He called his mom because I had talked to her about it.

Her advice was, "Yes, you need to go home."

He said, "Mom, did you tell Dolly she needed to go home?"

She answered, "Yes if she is trying to do the right thing, she needs to go home." He was so upset with her that night, but I think he knew what I needed to do deep down.

I told him, "I'll stay here tonight, but in the morning, I'm going home." He respected my stand.

The next morning was Sunday. I planned to leave for church and take all my stuff.

When I got up, he said, "I'm going to church with you."

I was like, "Don't go to church because of me."

He said, "I'm going, but Dicky Bishop Isaac Ross better not call me out."

My husband was a well-known drug dealer in the surrounding areas. I knew God had been dealing with him a few weeks prior. So much that, about three weeks before he went to church, he had stopped all illegal activities. Pastor Ross had lost his son in the streets due to violence and drugs. He had asked Marvin to join him on several occasions to advocate to the young boys in the streets; how ironic was that. The Bible says, God will use foolish things. Why would a known drug dealer be asked to talk to the community about drugs? God had a plan in motion; however, none of us knew the events that were about to transpire. We went to church that day. It was an awesome move of God. I was praising God. God was doing some cleansing, restoring, and sanctification in my life. I wanted to give everything to God, and I did. I opened my eyes and guess who was standing up in front of the church giving his life to the Lord? Yes, yours truly, Marvin.

I was thinking, *"He said yes!"* That's all I needed to hear.

He had previously given me an engagement ring. We already had the papers, but for some reason, until this moment, I couldn't do it. To make a long story short. We got married that same day at Pastor Ross's House; I just knew that this is it. We are gonna live happily ever after. At least, that's what I thought. I had been saved three weeks, and my knight in shining armor gave his life to the Lord.

The next three weeks were perfect. We went on vacation with our little blended family; we had an amazing weekend. Little did I know, our fairytale life was about to come to a screeching halt. There are times in life when you think things are going the way we plan. God will allow unexpected events to happen to throw us off the pier of life. That's when we have to trust Him.

HOW DO YOU TRUST GOD?

- Just like in a normal relationship, you have to know Him.
  (John 17:3, Philippians 3:10)
- What are God's Promises? (The word Of God)
  (John 16:33, Psalm 32:8)
- Having the confidence that God will not Harm you.
  (Jeremiah 29:11)
- Be willing to give God complete control of your life.
  (Job 12:10, John 15:5)
- Accept His will knowing that He knows you best.
  (Romans 12;2, John 17:3)

CHAPTER 2

Have You Tried My Servant

It is July 2, 1992; we had just returned from our vacation two days ago. It's around 7 am. A loud knock on the door woke me up. However, it was no normal knock. It was loud enough to wake a dead person. I went to the door. Before I could open it, I was forced back at gunpoint by the FBI Task Force too many to count. This was one of the scariest moments of my life. They raided the house and made all of us sit in one room while they were in the back bedroom, interrogating my husband.

I was thinking to myself, *"We're gonna be Ok. Marvin said he was done selling drugs, and I believe him."*

I was confident that they wouldn't find anything in the house. I figured they would do their search, find nothing, and leave. Keep in mind, we both were saved, and for about six weeks, Marvin was clean from selling drugs. I thought that we both are saved now; we were excited about our new life. God had forgiven us. So what was their problem? What we did not know is there had been months of investigation. Unlike God, they weren't gonna forgive him for his past criminal activity. There went my theory that if you give your life to Christ, He will fix everything, and everything in your life will fall in place. The reality was that all Satan imps put on their little red suits, got their pitchforks out, and found our address. Instead of falling in place, I felt like my life fell apart.

The Feds arrested Marvin; he was facing at least 7-15 years in Federal Prison. Delaware didn't have a Federal Prison, so he went to New Jersey.

"What am I supposed to do now?" I asked God, "not only am I a newlywed, but I'm a babe in Christ. I don't know the word because I never was a religious person. I don't know very much about faith."

"This just seems so unfair," I thought.

I expected Marvin and I to take our kids to church and grow in the Lord together; this was all new to me. God and I did a lot of talking.

I would visit Marvin in New Jersey 2-3 times a week while managing his business and mines. It was doing this time I began to develop a relationship with God. My faith grew, and I would ask God about everything. I fell in Love with Jesus. I often wonder if Marvin was home, would I have depended on God as I did. Probably not; I was so dependent on him that I would never have found out who Jesus was in His fullness.

Roman 8:28, And we know that all things work together

for good to those who love God.

Life was so stressful. I remember one day we both had reached our breaking point.

Marvin said, "You can get an annulment because we haven't been married that long."

Following all the drama, it sounded like a good idea at the time. However, after things cooled down, we thought about how much we loved each other and decided not to. I felt like I made not only a commitment to Marvin, but I also made a commitment to God. So, I decided to hang in there.

It was court date after court date and disappointment after disappointment. We would be at a high knowing that God was going to release him. Only to get in court to hear the judge say denied. Those rides home were the longest ever.

He would constantly remind me of **1 Corinthians 10:13, He will not put more on us than we can bear.**

I'm thinking, *"Lord, You must really be bragging on me because this seems unbearable."* Finally, almost two years later, he was released from prison.

In the Book of Job 1:8, God asks Satan, "Have you considered my servant Job?"

You may find yourself in an unfavorable position. Please

don't take it as a harsh punishment. God allows these things to happen.

Job 1:12, There is nothing Satan can do unless God allows.

Therefore, if He is allowing it, He has confidence that you can endure it. Through our test in life, we must remember that God knows us better than we know ourselves. He will use our trials as opportunities to develop us into vessels that will be effective in the kingdom of God. It's up to us to decide to give God permission to use us as an instrument to build.

1 Corinthians 6:19-20, Your body is the temple of God.

CHAPTER 3

Know Who You Are in God

You must realize there is nothing you can do to deserve the mercy and grace that covers you. However, realize that you are joint heirs in Christ.; we are His children. You can walk in the grace of God. Some provisions have been set before you. Don't let the devil convince you that you are under condemnation. Who the Son set free is free indeed.

Ephesians 2:10, For we are God's handiwork, created in Christ Jesus to do good works, which God prepared in advance for us to do.

You are not here by chance, but God formed you and created you for a purpose. We are in His image. My God that is a staggering thought! That I am the image of God. If only we could allow our finite minds to grab hold of an infinite God, there is nothing impossible with God.

Ephesians 3:20-21 says it perfectly, "Now to him who is able to do exceedingly abundantly above all that we can ask or think, according to the power that works in us."

That leaves us to respond to what power we are working in. God doesn't want us to walk inferior to this world because He gave us the power and authority to be victorious and not to become victim to our circumstances. Many Times people have departed this world full of purpose because they don't know who they are in Christ. I know this may be contrary to a lot of beliefs. Instead, they might say when it's my time; I will go.

My question would be…What has God assigned to you that you didn't accomplish?

What did you do with your talents?

Did you bury them, or did you let someone bewitch you?

Don't adapt and mold into the stereotype of what Christianity means to others. Seek God for the plans He has for you. I wouldn't want to live in a world of clones.

Everyone walks around dressed like me, talking like me, and think as I thought at times. You are a free creature. I'm learning to separate myself from people that would keep me entangled. It will become like a web that will strangle the life out of you. Learn to unweave yourself from this form of bondage. You will find freedom in Christ. When you find freedom, you will hear God's plan without all the clutter. It's wasn't until I was in a place in my life where I felt a brokenness that I had never felt before that I had to truly know who I was in God or walk around hopeless and in despair. That was the day that God let me know that the mantle He has placed on my life requires me not to mourn as others, which was a difficult thing to do. When He called the disciples, He told them to leave what they were doing and follow Him.

CHAPTER 4

An Intimate Relationship with God

This is one of the most important chapters of this book; having an intimate relationship with God. We can't begin to compare our relationships with any individual to our relationship with God. Why?

1. God is the only person that will love us unconditionally-**1 John 4:7-8, 2 Chronicles 6:14, Romans 8:31-32, Psalm 36:7** God's love is so agape that regardless of how low life may take you, His love will find you. God said, He will be with you; He will never leave you.

2. God is the only person that forgives us when our actions in man's eyes are unforgivable; God loves us so much that He sent His Son Jesus to redeem us from our sins. You may have been in a place in your life where your actions have been without an excuse. Jesus gave His life for you. Go to the Father with a repented heart, and your sins will be forgiven. Don't categorize your behavior thinking, but my sin is too great. Jesus' blood and God's love will cover our multitude of sins.

3. God is the only person that will never misunderstand you. **1 John 3:20, God is greater than our heart he knows everything.**

Psalms 139:4, Before the word is on our tongue, God already knows.

God will never misunderstand you. He knows us better than we know ourselves. So you never have to worry about Him not knowing your most intimate thoughts. He said, your thoughts are not My thoughts. He may change your plan because God knows us, and He knows what is best. Trust God and allow Him to guide you into a plan much greater than yours. Our lives are not our own. We are to reign under Him. That is the will of God for our life.

I'm going to be transparent because I pray that this book will help you. I desire that something I say will touch your spirit and empower you to be steadfast and unmovable, always abounding in the works of the Lord.

In the first years of my relationship with God, my spiritual life was unstable. I treated God the same way I treated a man. If things went according to the way I expected then He was awesome. However, if things went south, I would get in my feelings or stop in my tracks. I'm so glad in the midst of my ignorance; God still showered me with His love, His grace, and His mercy.

Lamentations 3:22-23, God will allow us to mature in His

mercies.

He is not a God that follows us around with a rod in His hand, ready to tap our fingers every time we make a mistake. He is a God of love.

He said in **Matthew 23:37, How He long to gather His children together as a hen gathers her chicks under her wings, and you were not willing.**

Look at God's mercy. He loved me when I couldn't love myself. When I looked at my past, all my faults and failures, Jesus' blood was able to wash them clean. When I didn't see my future, He assured me of the plans He has for me.

Jeremiah 29:11, Plans that I prosper, plans to not harm me, and plans to give me hope. This is the God I chose to serve and spend my life in an intimate relationship.

CHAPTER 5

Will You Go?

The question God asks us is, "Will you go?"

Luke 14:23, Master told his servant to go into the highways...

After being saved a few years, God began to deal with me about the call God had on my life.

I kept hearing the question, "What is God calling you to do?"

My answer was, "I don't know." I remember in one dream I had; I was ministering.

I was thinking, *"Not me. I could never do that."*

I was a quiet person when I got into a crowd. I felt like I did not speak well and definitely not to a group of people. It was one sign after another until finally, I told God and Him only, yes. But evidently, God did not keep good secrets because everywhere I went, people would say the Lord told me you're an Evangelist. I was like, Ok, God, I hear You loud and clear.

I asked myself, *"Why was it so hard to accept the call?"* There were several reasons:

Reasons we don't accept the call:

- **Fear**
- **Feeling unworthy**

- **Feeling inadequate**
- **Immature**
- **Worrying about what people say**
- **I'm going to wait for the right time**

These are just some of the reasons that made me hesitant to accept the call of God on my life. What are some of your excuses?

Philippians 4:13-17, States that we can do all things through Christ, which strengthens us.

You don't have to fear. God will never give us an assignment and then leave us to accomplish it on our own. I use this as a safety net. Whenever God gives me an assignment, I turn it back into His hands and say, God, this is Your assignment; I am just the vessel. Ask God to show you His plan for your life. He will use your passions, your history, and your gifts to mold and design a ministry that will allow you to be effective for the kingdom of God.

Everyone that has a relationship with God should be continually seeking Him daily for directions by praying, fasting, and meditating in His word. I once had a good idea about how to do a ministry. It had been set into action.

I remember the Holy Spirit speaking to me, saying, *"Is it a good idea, or is that what I told you to do?"* It is very important to know what God is saying.

If we go on our good ideas, it could lead to a road of disaster and leaving debris behind us. Many of my life failures have arrived from stepping out on my own opinions or allowing others' ideas or opinions to guide me. Instead of seeking God about what to do, I made hasty or foolish judgments, and I have the debris in my life that I am now trying to rebuild. It's not too late. Don't you give up. God has a way of turning those things around for our good. **Romans 8:28.**

CHAPTER 6

It Will Cost You Something

Paul is one of my favorite characters in the Bible. He's my favorite because of the power of his transformation (from killing Christians to becoming one). It lets me know that no matter what road you travel, the blood of Jesus can wash you and use for God's glory. It also could be because I can relate to the hardship that Paul had to endure. So much hardship that Paul asked God to take the thorn from his flesh. How many times have you gone through trial after trial until you got to a place where you ask God to take it away. Jesus asked His Father to take this cup from me when He was on the cross, sacrificing His life for you and me. I have been in several situations when I ask God to take this away. I can't endure it anymore. Each time the Holy Spirit would take me by my hand, and a few times, He had to carry me through. We have to be willing to go through the fire, knowing that when we get to the other side, the glory of God will shine through us. Our life should be a living testimony of keeping the power of God. Here is my testimony of how God sustained me through the fire.

Over the years, I have gone through so many trials. As I look back, I know it was God's grace that gave me the strength to make it through. When I think about my life, the poem that talks about the 'footprints in the sand' comes to my mind. When the person asked Jesus why there were only two footprints in the sand instead of four, and Jesus said, *"That is because I was carrying you."*

In this series, I will talk about the events in my life in the last three years, when it was nothing but God that carried me.

On October 6, 2016, I was at my salon, finishing my last client for the weekend. I got a phone call. On the other end was a lady telling me that there had been a bad accident; It was my son, Marvin. He was off at college playing football for Cheyney University in New Jersey; this was his third year. The lady explained how serious the accident was, and I needed to get there as soon as possible.

The stranger on the phone said, "I will stay with your son until you get here."

This woman didn't know me from a can of paint. God had sent them to watch over my son. I called my daughter Chrystal, and within minutes, we were on the road.

She asked me, "Mom, do you want me to drive?"

I said, "No."

It was something inside of me that felt like I needed to be

behind the wheel. I had to be in control of this situation. In the past, as long as I was in control of the situation, I could fix it. We got there so quickly I don't even remember most of the ride or any of the conversations. My mind was racing 100 miles an hour, unsure of what was going to be there to face me. My husband just happened to have a meeting in Wilmington that day, so he was only 20 minutes away from the hospital they took my son to. I was like 2 ½ hours away.

He kept calling me, asking, "Where are you? Get here as soon as you can." I know he called me at least ten times. That made me nervous.

I thought, *"Maybe he didn't want to give me the worst news on the phone."*

When I pulled up in the ER parking lot, there was the couple that had called me about the accident. They waved for me to get out and go inside; they said they would park the car.

I was thinking to myself, *"This is bad."*

When I walked into the room where they had my son, I looked at him, and my heart dropped, but at the same time, I was relieved. He was alive. He was so injured from the outer appearance.

I was thinking, *"That's Ok, a little TLC, and he would be*

fine."

He had to be sent to Jefferson Memorial because the hospital he was at was not advanced enough to treat him. He was told he had a spine injury.

I was thinking, *"Ok, we can fix that."*

When we got to John Hopkins, we found out his spine was completely severed; this news was devastating. As a mother, I wasn't concerned about myself. My concern was how Marvin was gonna handle the doctor's report. I remember the look in his eyes and the sound of his weeping that I'd never heard before. I got angry with God. I questioned God, "Why my son?" I know that question may have seemed selfish.

A few weeks later, I had one of the biggest assignments to minister. How can I minister about a God that had my son in a rehabilitation center fighting for his future? How was I gonna stand up and tell people that my God is a healer? One day He spoke to me so clearly and said, "He is alive." I broke down and repented asking God to forgive me. Some mother lost her child, and mine is still here.

The road of recovery has been rough and, at times, frustrating. But I know it's by the grace of God that he is still here. There was a part that I didn't tell you about. How could I leave that out?

While my son was pinned under the SUV truck. A man appeared and helped two other men pull him out from the truck. It was seconds before the SUV caught on fire. Witnesses said the man disappeared as quickly as he had appeared. No one could explain where this third-person went, and only two people saw him. I know God sent that angel to rescue my son for a reason.

He is doing amazing. I am astonished by the strength that God has given him. He has passed the doctor reports, and we are believing God for complete healing. I'm not going to say I know why it happened to make it look like I got this thing patented. He will allow things to happen, and we don't always understand, but we can trust Him through the process. I said a lot happened in the past three years.

Six months later, my business partner decided that she no longer wanted to be in a partnership. She just walks out. My business was already under strain, but I decided to continue to try to make it work. By this time, I was an emotional wreck. I was still praying when I could.

I would say to God, "Please see my heart because right now, I have nothing to say. I'm at the end of my rope. What else could happen?" Never ask God that question.

Six months after the episode with my partner walking out, we had an electrical fire at our house. One night we were sleeping. I heard pounding on my bedroom window. My son's friend came running into our bedroom, yelling, "The house is on fire!" She grabbed my granddaughter Peyton and helped my son out. When I jumped up, the house was in flames. I ran to the top of the stairs to wake up my daughter Shelita and her two kids London and Lorenz. I remember feeling the heat from the flames. This was like a dream. I went to the other bedroom and grabbed my other grandson Khayne which later vomited because of the smoke inhalation. It was like we were in a movie. Everyone escaped the burning house safely.

My mind was so confused I was thinking, *"Is everyone out?"* Thank God we made it.

The guy that was knocking on my window to wake us up that night was a neighbor. We were in the yard across the street, watching almost everything we owned go up in flames. Our neighbor came over to check on us. He told us he saw the fire and ran over. Then he introduced himself. He said his name is Gabriel. Yes! Gabriel like the angel. We lived in this house for two years, and I never knew this man's name. I thought that was God's way of saying. I sent My angel once again. The fire left us homeless for five months. During this time, we experience the love of so many people. God always provided by giving us favor. We always had a place to be safe and lay our head. It wasn't home, but it was shelter. God continued to show up or send His angels to look after us. Doors opened, and we found a place we called home.

Finally, things began to level out. I was so emotionally and physically drained. The Holy Spirit had told me months before the fire to downsize; I decided to close my business. I went to another salon to work. None of these salon decisions made sense to me. I did what I felt God was saying because I wanted to be obedient to Him. Now, it all makes sense; the Pandemic came. If I were still in my own business, I would not have been able to survive financially. God loves us, so if we continue to seek Him and listen to that small still voice, God will lead us into a place of safety.

2020 came in; January came in like a lion. On January 9th, I received a phone call. My father had a heart attack. They said he had survived, but would need surgery. I went to the hospital. Dad reassured me that he would be fine. We spent a couple of days together. I found out a lot of things about him that I didn't know. We were so much alike. We even liked the same TV shows. It was so funny watching him yell out the answers to Family Feud (my favorite show). My father had not been in my life for many years. There were years in my life that I was angry, not understanding why my dad was not there for me. It's true that they say when a father is not in their daughter's life that it may leave a void or inadequacy. I felt like something was wrong with me that he was not there.

About 8-years-ago, I decided to forgive my father for not being there. I made a conscious effort to develop a relationship with him. I now realize that the decision had a lot to do with the relationship that was enhancing with my Heavenly Father. The Holy Spirit told me that my dad did what he knew to do. I am so glad that we had developed a good relationship. I would look up, and there he would be.

He would say, "Hey Baby, I just dropped by to see how you were." The little girl in me would melt.

The last time he visited me was about a month before he had a heart attack. He came to the salon and just sat there. He was so quiet that day.

I asked him, "Dad, are you Ok?"

He said, "Yeah, I'm just sitting here watching you." Then he got up and gave me one of those bear hugs that only he could give and said, "I love You."

I left the hospital on the 11th, not knowing that it would be our last conversation that we would have. My father died. The pain of losing a parent is something that I will never have the words to express. God gave me peace, knowing my dad was saved, but the pain was still there. It took months for me to realize that I will never talk to my dad again in this earthly vessel.

Several months went by. The governor made a mandate that all salons are to be closed due to the coronavirus. For the first time, it hit me that this virus was something we had never seen before. People overnight lost their jobs and their businesses. I had heard about COVID-19; however, I never imagined how contagious it was, like most people. I had no clue of the devastation and pain it would cause to my family.

In May, my mother became sick with flu-like symptoms. She was back and forth with virtual doctor appointments. I never understood how you could diagnose COVID on the phone. Finally, after three weeks, my son Tasario took her to the hospital, and she was admitted. We found out that it was COVID. The hard part of the virus is that the hospital wouldn't allow us to be with her.

My mother was an amazing woman. She loved her family. I look at how she mothered me as an only child. She was my shero.

I never remember wanting anything. If I could be half the mother she was, I would be a successful parent. She made me feel safe even when her life was in danger.

When she went in the hospital, I was thinking, *"Ok...they will treat her, and she will be fine."*

After two days, I thought she should be getting better; instead, she was getting worse. On Mother's Day, I spoke to her, and she was so exhausted. I was beginning to get worried by now. My mom is strong; this can't happen. By day 3, my mom had to be put on the ventilator. I made all kinds of promises to God if He would heal her. I prayed every prayer and read all the right scriptures. I thought of every reason why God couldn't let this happen.

After a week passed, the doctor called me to come to the hospital because they said she would not survive. On the way there, the Holy Spirit spoke to me and said, *"Your mom want you to know that she is Ok and that she has seen a glimpse of glory."* She was in her condition, but she summoned the Holy Spirit to tell me that she was Ok. That is the kind of love that God demonstrates to us daily.

It's the third week. After begging God to heal her, I heard the Holy Spirit again speak clearly, saying, *"I'm not gonna do it."*

I fell on my knees, weeping like a baby, "God, please Don't take my mom!" She fought for a week after that.

The Lord woke me up around 2:30 am, saying, *"It's time to let go."*

I said, "God, if you're going to take her, please don't make me have to decide to take her off the ventilator." I don't think I could live with the pain if I had to make that decision.

Around 2:45 am on June 8th; I got the phone call saying your mother has passed. After four weeks on the ventilator, she died. When I looked at the death certificate, the time of death was 2:30 am. We were so connected; I believe that at 2:30 am I felt her heart stop beating. My heart will never be the same. I will not go through any more details because my heart breaks every time I think about the loss of my best friend. The person that loved me more than she loved herself.

The Holy Spirit reminded me of how my mother had developed an intimate relationship with God like never before. She was my biggest supporter. She was at almost everything that concerned me.

In the few months before her getting sick, I heard her cry out to God in a new realm. I know now that was God preparing her to be with Him. This experience has left me numb. When I was preparing her funeral, I tried to decide who could express who she was in the depth of who she was.

The Holy Spirit asked me, *"Who knows her better than you? Minister her eulogy?"*

I said to God, "You got to be kidding me. How am I supposed to do that? I haven't even healed from my father's death, and now you want me to minister my mom's funeral?"

You know how we talk to God like He doesn't know how we feel.

He said, *"My grace is sufficient for thee."*

God has given me the peace of knowing my mother is Ok. Do I understand? NO! However, I put my trust in God so that I will trust the process. When there is an empty space in your heart, God wants you to fill it with more of Him. Don't waste your time being angry or bitter towards God. He created you, and He knows everything that concerns you.

THE CONCLUSION

These are some of the numerous times in my life that I know without a doubt that it was God that was and still is carrying me. There were times that I felt so weak that I was afraid I would collapse from exhaustion. I would tell God I have nothing left to give. I knew I wasn't gonna turn my back on God, but I have nothing left to give. I remember one day crying dealing with my mother's death.

Holy Spirit said, *"Go in the room and cry, but when you get done crying, come out with your head up."* I was upset about that.

"How can a loving God be so cold?" I thought.

He later let me know that the assignment He has on my life doesn't allow me time to mourn as others.

He said, *"I assured you that your mother is Ok. Your assignment is to make sure others are Ok when I call. When you tell Me you have nothing else to give, that's when I will fill you with power. When you say you feel like you're gonna collapse, that's when I Will Carry You.*

God loves us so much that He gave His Son so that you and I can have eternal life. No matter where we are, He is there. I find safety in knowing that I house the Holy Spirit. He trusts me with such a precious and valuable gift. There is no greater love. I will end this book with the thought of GOD CARRYING YOU, carrying you through your hurt, through your pain, and out of your shame. Tap into the gifts and the unlimited treasures that await you in the presence of God. There is nothing that can overtake you when you abide in that secret place with the Father. God has so much He wants to reveal to us. Unfortunately, sometimes these revelations come with a cost. In order to reign with Him, the Bible says, we will have some suffering, but the suffering does not compare to the glory that will be revealed. Walk with your head held high, my sister, and my brother; you are not defeated, but you are victorious in God!

THE CUP THAT YOU DRINK FROM WILL GIVE YOU ETERNAL LIFE AND ETERNAL LIFE FOR OTHERS.

AMEN.

ABOUT THE AUTHOR

Prophetess Dolly Morris

Prophetess Dolly Morris was born on April 26, 1964. She was born to Lula M. Martin and George Fletcher in the small town in Crisfield, Maryland. She is an only child.

In 1992, she married Marvin Morris Jr. She has Five Children Tasario Martin, Chrystal Martin, Marvin Morris 3rd, Shelita Morris, and Marshona Morris. Prophetess Morris gave her life to Christ in 1992.

In 1997, she was ordained under the COG in Cleveland Tn. She has been a member of the Booker St Church Of God for 26 years under the leadership of her father in-law Bishop Marvin Morris Sr., and Mother in-law First Lady Lorriane Morris.

Prophetess Dolly Morris has been an entrepreneur for over 30 years in the beauty industry. Her passion has always been to beautify the woman from outside.

She realized that it didn't matter how much the outside beauty shined, many of these women were hurt and broken on the inside. That's when God gave her the dream that gave birth to the vision of Women Birthing A Nation. An organization for women that need a support system.

God also gave her a ministry called Soaking In God's Presence. This event allows women to experience an intimate encounter with the Father. She is a minister, a prophetess counselor, a teacher, a motivational speaker, an author, a mother, and a wife. The most precious title she holds is being a child of the Most High King Jesus Christ.

DOLLY AND HER PRECIOUS MOTHER LULA

November 3, 1947 to June 8, 2020

My mother was a victim of COVID-19. However, I know she is in the loving arms of my Father. Therefore, this gives me comfort. My mom was my BEST FRIEND, and she will be DEARLY MISSED!

REST IN PEACE, MOM, I LOVE YOU!

www.ingramcontent.com/pod-product-compliance
Lightning Source LLC
Chambersburg PA
CBHW062206100526
44589CB00014B/1972